Miracle
A Parent's Blessing
A Newborn Baby
Memories and Milestones

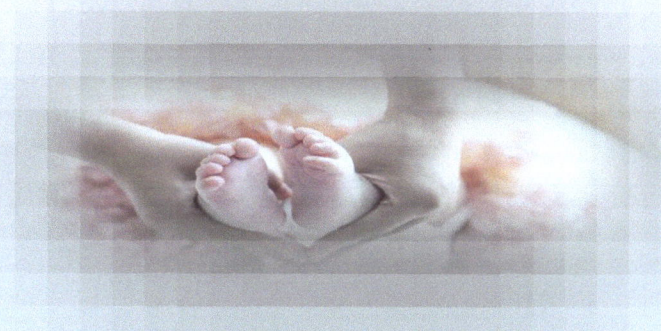

Jessie Hionis

Miracle
A Parent's Blessing
A Newborn Baby

"No doubt about it: children are a gift from the Lord;

the fruit of the womb is a divine reward."

Psalm 127:3-4

Dedicated to my miracle, George, without whom,
life could never be as precious!

Copyright © 2023 Jessie Hionis All rights reserved

The characters and events portrayed in this book are fictitious. Any similarity to real persons, living or dead, is coincidental and not intended by the author.

No part of this book may be reproduced, or stored in a retrieval system, or transmitted in any form or by any means, electronic, mechanical, photocopying, recording, or otherwise, without express written permission of the publisher.

Photos: Pixabay

Miracle

We couldn't wait to see your face,
to hold you in our arms.

To hold you tight, To kiss your cheek,
To shelter you from harm.

*As time grew close, and every day,
impatiently we waited.*

*For you to come,
look in our eyes,
to see what God created.*

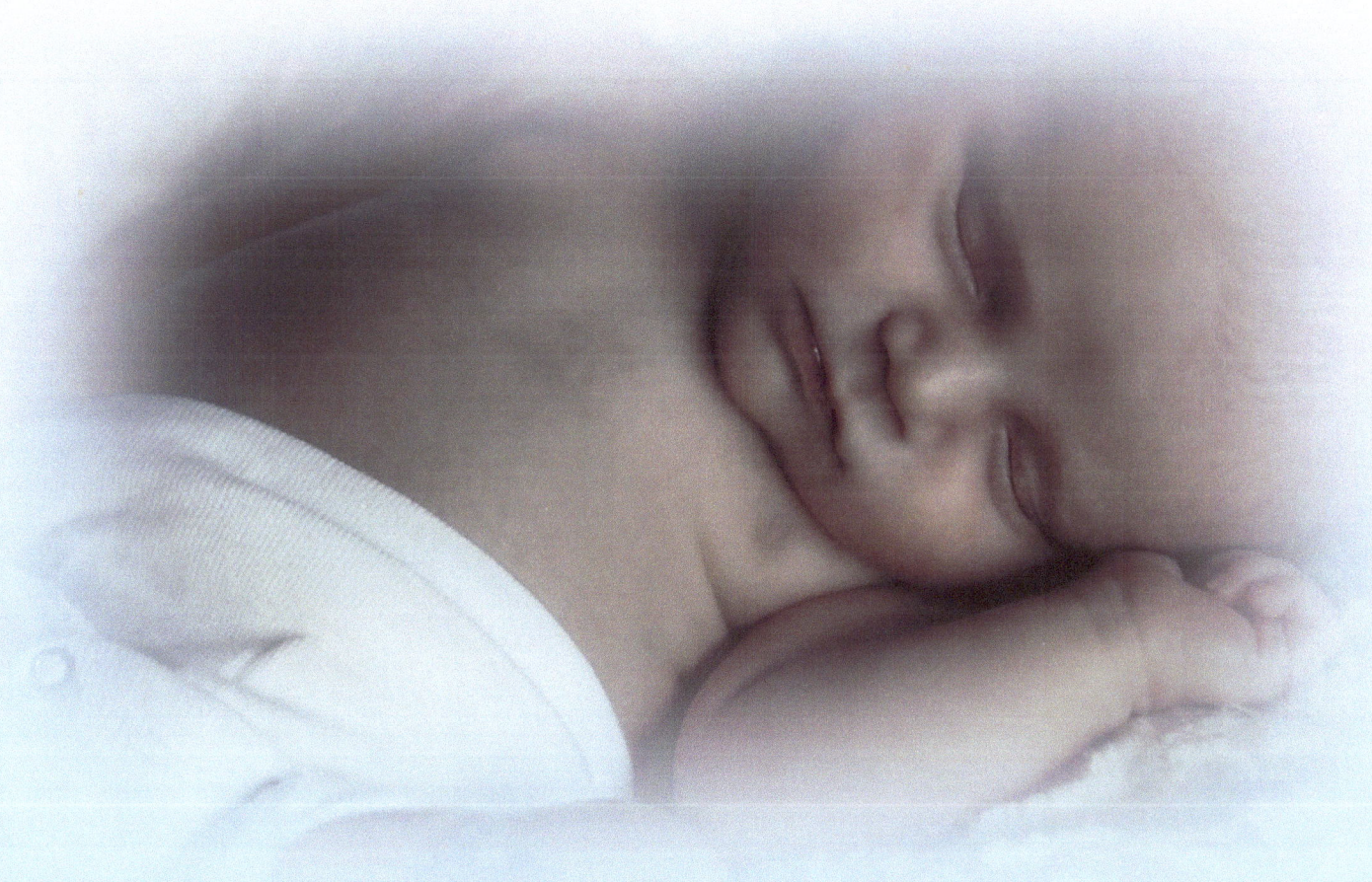

A miracle has blessed our lives,
And made our dreams come true.

Your beating heart, your precious smile, that miracle is you!

Memories and Milestones

The Planning for the baby? How long? Feelings? Thoughts? Memories? Experiences?

Memories and Milestones

The News: When did you learn that you were going to have a baby? Date? Place? Feelings? Thoughts? Memories? Experiences?

Memories and Milestones

The Pregnancy: Medical appointments? Meetings? Books and articles read? Thoughts? Memories? Experiences?

Memories and Milestones

The Preparation: What did you buy, make or receive for the baby? Feelings? Thoughts? Memories? Experiences?

Memories and Milestones

The Arrival: Delivery? Time? Place? Height and weight of baby? Feelings? Memories?

Memories and Milestones
The First Week: Weight? Height? Feelings? Thoughts? Memories? Experiences?

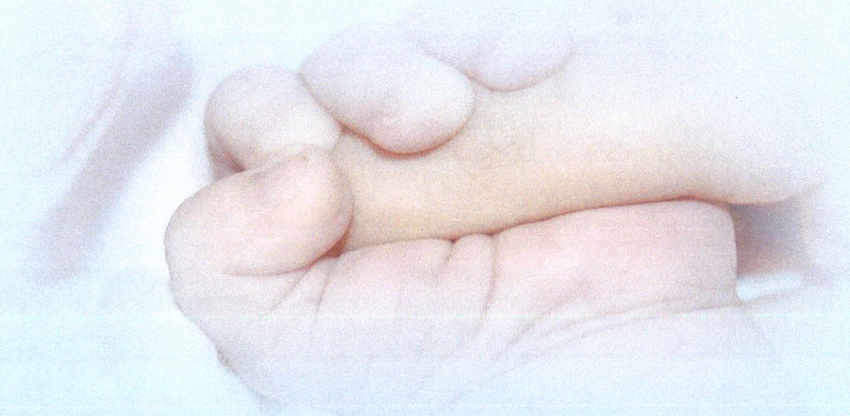

Memories and Milestones
The Second Week: Weight? Height? Feelings? Thoughts? Memories? Experiences?

Memories and Milestones

The Third Week: Weight? Height? Feelings? Thoughts? Memories? Experiences?

Memories and Milestones

The First Month: Weight? Height? Feelings? Thoughts? Memories? Experiences?

Memories and Milestones

At Three Months: Weight? Height? Feelings? Thoughts? Memories? Experiences?

Memories and Milestones

At Six Months: Weight? Height? Feelings? Thoughts? Memories? Experiences?

Memories and Milestones

At One Year: Weight? Height? Feelings? Thoughts? Memories? Experiences?

Memories and Milestones

Baby's Firsts: Smile? Laughs? Sleep through the night? Sitting up? Standing Up? Crawls? Steps? Words? Eating solid food?

Memories and Milestones

Celebrations: Baby shower: (Where? Organizers? When?) Christening or baptism?: (Where? When? Cost?) Birthday party? (Where? When? Guests?)

Memories and Milestones

A Message To Your Adult Baby. Your memories, thoughts and feelings.

www.ingramcontent.com/pod-product-compliance
Lightning Source LLC
LaVergne TN
LVHW071654060526
838200LV00029B/454